Australian alphabet

Other poetry volumes by Timoshenko Aslanides:

The Greek connection (1977)
Passacaglia and fugue (1979)
One hundred riddles (1984)
Australian things (1990)

… and guide books, with Jenny Stewart:

Goulburn and environs, a comprehensive guide (1983)
Canberra and the Australian Capital Territory (1988)

Australian alphabet

Timoshenko Aslanides

Publication assisted by the Australia Council, the Australian Government's arts funding and advisory body.

 *Butterfly Books*

© Copyright Timoshenko John Aslanides, 1992.
All rights reserved. No part of this publication may be reproduced, stored in a retrieval system or transmitted in any form or by any means, electronic, mechanical, photocopying, facsimile, recording or otherwise, without the prior written permission of the author and the publisher.

First published in 1992 by
Butterfly Books
P.O. Box 107
Springwood
New South Wales 2777
Australia.

National Library of Australia Cataloguing-in-Publication data:

Aslanides, Timoshenko John, 1943–
  Australian alphabet.

ISBN 0 947333 52 5.

I. Title.

A821.3

Cover design Kevin Drumm.

Typeset in Times by Butterfly Books.

Printed in Australia by
  Star Printery Pty. Limited, Erskineville, New South Wales.

for Jenny

Acknowledgements

To my wife, Jenny Stewart, who supported me while I planned, read for and, during 1988 and 1989, wrote this book.

To the following magazines and newspapers, in which the majority of these poems were previously published: *Antipodes* (New York), *Blast, The Canberra Times, Imago, LiNQ, Northern Perspective, Otis Rush, Quadrant, Redoubt, Southerly, The Sydney Morning Herald, Westerly*.

For the illustrations to the Quadrilles:
To *The heads of the people* (7 August 1847) for the drawing of the Flying Pieman;
To *The Bulletin* (10 December 1892) for the cartoon by Livingstone Hopkins.

Foreword

TIMOSHENKO ASLANIDES WAS a student of mine in the Department of Music at Sydney University in 1965. I well remember that his compositions were the best in the class. His lyric gift was obvious, and he has since become an original creator in the one art form, poetry, which most nearly approaches and which for millennia has been most closely associated with music.

Australian alphabet is Tim's sixth book of poetry. It is peopled with Australians who, wherever born, have been and still are important to us. So, in poems whose titles often seem selected for their Australian resonance, Tim reintroduces us to Andrew 'Boy' Charlton, John Batman, Ben Chifley, Caroline Chisholm, Charles Conder, Dan Deniehy, Lawrence Hargrave, Fred McCubbin, John Macarthur, Nellie Melba, and 'Long Bob' Spears, among many others. By associating himself and his concerns with these Australians and their concerns, Tim has produced a poetic counterpoint to, and commentary on, contemporary Australian life which I find compelling. He does this with rhythmical and lyrical language, humour, and that obvious sense of enjoyment in his work that one expects from an artist with something to say.

One of the poems makes reference to me as one of a number of Australians who have had an influence on Tim's work; certainly I believe that in this and in previous books he himself is an influence upon others.

These artistically complex but disarmingly simple and accessible poems deserve the wide readership they will obtain, especially among those Australians who, sensing the irrelevance of European modes of thought in contemporary Australia, want to listen to the resonances of a lyric poetry which celebrates what has made, and continues to make us, what we are.

Peter Sculthorpe
Sydney, 1990

Contents

Foreword ... vii

Advertisement ... *1*
Barcoo Rot ... *3*
Confidence ... *5*
Death ... *7*
Ethics ... *11*
Fire ... *15*
Green ... *17*
Happiness ... *19*
Imagination ... *21*
Jenny ... *23*
Kenosis ... *24*
Letter (an appeal) ... *26*
Manly ... *29*
Nouns and colonial verbs ... *30*
Other ... *32*
Poetry ... *34*
Quadrilles ... *35*
    1 — The Collingwood Tote ... *35*
    2 — The Flying Pieman ... *37*
    3 — The Speaker's Mace ... *39*
Requiem ... *40*
Saturday ... *41*
Tradition ... *42*
Unless ... *43*
Vegemite ... *44*
Women ... *45*
X-roads ... *47*
Yass ... *50*
Zeitgeist ... *52*
    My life so far ... *52*
    Your life so far ... *57*
    The relevance of everything ... *60*
    Salute ... *61*

Notes ... 63
Bibliography ... 75

Advertisement

Νίψον ἀνομήματα μὴ μόναν ὄψιν

I

It's no accident that I lead the Australian alphabet:
    an 'Aslan' is a lion and, though not
a native, symbol of my share of the Muses' largesse.
    They were nine as I am now: questions
from landscape at and under my hand. Let me explain: 5
    when I was young, we entertained each other
and ourselves: 'My first is in that, but never in this,
    my second's read twice when she writes me a kiss ...'
and so on 'till you spelt-out the answer.
    Let me begin by riddling my alphabet,   10
the basis and the glory of this book and name.
    My first is in wheat, then hay and, in place, the sound
of horses ready to race. I've never had to line-up, though,
    where an alphabet controlled a beginning.

II

Kids, I've read, on the other side of 'm', who waited   15
    for teachers to tick off their days, and then, as adults,
for officials to tick off their years, have blood-pressure and ulcers.
    My second letter is silent, for me as for you.
My third is in will, but not in 'may be', 'perhaps', 'I can try',
    'why don't you?' My fourth is in back, but not in front,   20
though again I lead my kind. My fifth is not 'beneath dignity';
    if Brahe didn't dig because he thought it 'infra dig',
then that delinquent attitude cost Burke and Wills their lives.

1

My sixth is in itself, and wellnigh everything.
My seventh is in death, but not in life, 25
   and stays with God, regardless of my prayers.
My eighth is a vowel, penultimate in plurals, possessives,
   participles, adverbs and those substantives,
('summer', 'travel', 'women') you don't have to learn to love.
   My ninth in the Greek is almost an abbreviation, 30
an afterthought added to a recollection, a squiggle
   that disappears down the page as Cooper's Creek
sinks into sand when a monsoon has blown itself inside out
   on the Diamantina, good Greek-Australian river.

III

As a capital, I summarise, being as elegant 35
   as the hammerbeam roof in St Saviour's, Goulburn
(this both defies gravity and rejects its arguments),
   or as dramatic as the walk into Agia Sophia,
when your breath pulls in and you know you have to admit, and admit.
   I remembered the palindrome carved upon the font, 40
the breach in the walls and the postern gate betrayed,
   before the rush, the slaughter, and burning of the books.
'Wash away your sins, not just the dirt on your face.'
   I leave the palindrome for another road,
and decide I don't need an advertising agency: 45
   'An Australian is anyone with a line
of me in memory' should satisfy the most fast-
   idious Trade Practices Legislation.

Barcoo Rot

I

Anything can 'make you want to spew': our
    disease of choice is the Barcoo Rot,
and shearers were especially susceptible:
    standing up, they couldn't hold down food
in the dragging bending clipping bleeding pushing, next-one,   5
    heat: the springtime it brings on much more than the shearing.
The rot set in like a long Monsoon and stayed, attaching
    like the Devil to anyone unsure of right
and wrong: fingers hands, taken-for-granted feet:
    no organ or activity was immune.   10
Left untreated, Barcoo Rot can addle the brain:
    why else was Governor Bligh apparently under
that bed at Major Johnston's coup? 'Will the Major
    go away if I pretend he isn't here?

II

Can a government that can't be found be seized?   15
    Where is that letter which damns "The Perturbator?",
That, also, was Barcoo Rot: when you don't know
    you have this disease, like love you've got it bad.
Brooding is a form of Barcoo Rot, a feeling that
    you should have replied when someone put you down: 20
the most damaging anger is directed at oneself, though luckless
    others take the brunt of unfocussed rage.
People who dream of punishing people only punish
    themselves: Samuel Marsden had the Barcoo Rot,
and Parramatta is his scar; Alfred Stephen hanged   25
    Mary Ann Brownlow; Redmond Barry had it too,
and though they called it 'carbuncle', Ned Kelly knew
    differently, and prophesied that judge's fate.

III
I found the Barcoo itself immune: when it runs,
    southwest Queensland, broadly, is its course   30
and South Australia, also broadly, its destination.
    I saw it snaked around its Coolabah and grass,
buried in wrapped-frog quiet beneath flaking jigsaw pieces
    of July, thick and hard as dinner plates.
I took one home to join those other souvenirs,   35
    the knick-knacks that may, but never do, come in handy.
Then one day it was gone. No one, no thing, this time,
    was witness, but I guess that Jenny threw it out,
and justifiably: it is a form of Barcoo Rot
    to put aside what was not lost when found.   40
All I remember now is a pancake-size piece
    of Queensland mud that might have roared through channel
country where good or bad luck puts you in the Georgina,
    Diamantina, the Thompson or the Cooper,
or, caked on a car, takes you to Oodnadatta,   45
    which they'll tell you was made by the Devil
himself when, suffering the Barcoo Rot, he threw
    at the town those stones that now surround it.

Confidence

'Ask questions. Then ask more questions. Then ask,
    "Is there a question I haven't asked?"' That's
the advice I gave, though I didn't always follow it myself
    — that takes confidence, and the getting of that
is the getting of everything. 'I'll start slow', said Andrew,
    'Boy' Charlton of his race with Arne Borg,
'but watch me finish.' Dozens climbed the trees; hundreds
    stood-up best in boats; ten thousand crowded
Saturday Sydney's Domain Pool, shouting the only
    way you can for the eleven minutes they swam
880 yards: with the unselfconsciousness that
    always photographs as a suspension
of decibels in so many open mouths, the hands
    raised as much to pump the lungs as to balance
the feet stamping for our champion, his record,
    and our win against the world and that inevitable
comparison, Sweden. 'Can I help you out of the water?'
    my despairing teacher said, dropping his arms
along with his hope that I'd ever learn to swim and catch
    the rest of the class. Then I knew that to be ten
and thin and determined to swim constituted confidence.
    Excellence in champions may be talent and work,
but they, too, have to start. 'Can I try once more?' I asked
    and did; and did. In learning to swim, as with riding
a bike, you remember where, when and who taught you.
    Not tall, not short, still my legs were smaller
then in proportion to the rest of me, and for this
    I dropped my bicycle seat to ride around
my clean, suburban Cabramatta. "Long Bob" Spears,
    by contrast, had legs so long that still the seat
was raised on his built-for built-up bicycle. 'Who is
    "Long Bob" Spears?', the Americans asked.
'Although called an Australian, Spears is American',

they also replied, never having heard
of Dubbo, best 'red earth' farming country in New South Wales,
    and breeder of Australian cycling wonders.
Paris, Bordeaux, Milan and Turin Grand Prixs,
    world championship, gold medals,
fees, sponsorships and that formal insouciance
    that European presidents, kings
and queens affect in the presence of a real monarch,
    a true ruler of the velodrome: these
his rewards. The world can be generous to a champion
    generous to rivals and confident in capacities.
My confidence is that of a 44 year,
    67 kilogram, 165
centimetre crown-bald, short-bearded, glasses-wearing poet
    who once thought himself a composer.
But my first symphony, which lasted three minutes,
    had only as many ideas; my violin concerto,
doubly scratchy, was destroyed with my string quartet.
    No loss: I could still play Beethoven,
a storm which suited my youth, or later, Mozart, and a lucid
    elegance of piano apparently made
for middle age and its simplifying, clearer textures,
    and concentration of relationships;
for the dropping-off of detritus of years of harmonic fill-in,
    the pretence of modulation mere enharmonic
change, the waiting and the making-do. Make-power,
    confidence, thought and feeling are in
a more-nearly perfect balance now, like the strings, brass,
    woodwind and percussion in a well-conducted
orchestra, or the fruit, acid, tannin and oak
    in a well-made wine. The touch, surer now
than it ever was, is also accumulating handfuls
    of answers, most of which appear to have life
as the perennial question. I expect to find those
    remaining relate to the confidence needed to live it.

Death

I — Light on the past

It was an obvious question: was he dead on
    arrival at Canberra Community Hospital?
I rang. 'Hold on; I'll check', and shoes echoed the shine
    of polished linoleum down an admin-
istration corridor, dropping decibels
    with the years: 54, 53, 52:
'We can't say', she said. 'Admission records before
    August 1951 were destroyed
in a fire', and I didn't disbelieve her, but a voice,
    not my own, disagreed; I held again
(it was as if there were a chance he was still alive):
    'No;' she said, 'the records were destroyed
in a flood.' And I tried to imagine the Molonglo River
    pouring through the hospital, pushing
nurses, doctors, and patients comatose on trolleys
    through swing doors that otherwise kiss
behind you when you visit, the turbid swirling water
    threatening mud packs in the plaster dressings,
while breakfast trays floated through broken windows to
    the inevitable seagulls on the lake,
argumentative as ever about the quality of hospital food.
    It wasn't real. Then I connected the two:
First the fire, then the 'flood' from fire hoses!
    I thanked her and asked the Archives anyway.
They wrote: 'burst water pipe', adding, routinely, that
    'a leaflet on your rights of appeal' was enclosed.
And again I didn't disbelieve, but then I thought:
    Why can't I have a prime minister
like that? Why do the best people always die

so long ago? Did the past have monopoly
on goodness? Of course I'd appeal. To parliament. I rang.
   The new one, on the hill. 'Yes;' they said,
'we can show you his room in the Hotel Kurrajong',
   room A1, ground floor, probably,
near the dining room, with easy access to favourite
   corned beef, and potatoes cooked in their jackets.
It seemed reasonable, though myself I'd have preferred
   the room above, but ruled it out because
of double stairs. I wouldn't climb anything
   with a heart like that in 1951.
Or go to a Jubilee Ball. In fact, I've never liked
   such parties, the formal dancing, the butterfly
conversations that left bits of you in corners of every
   room, bits you had to gather before
you left, or else you weren't complete. The remembering
   which glass was yours, how many you'd had of what,
when and with whom; whether, having had too much
   or not enough, you made — or didn't make —
some commitment, later called on and required.
   You always regret and think of friends, or books.

II — Light on a room and a process

They built the Kurrajong in '26, the year
   that Spearfelt won the Cup, and electric trains
ran Sydney through to Oatley; when Pavlova danced for Melbourne,
   Chaliapin sang, and Backhous played our pleasure.
When Twofold Bay closed its telescopes on whales,
   and Mt Stromlo opened them on stars.
In this capital, the *Canberra Times* had, correctly,

announced its birth, but got this death quite wrong:
he wasn't 'working in his room'; he was in bed.
  Phyllis lay beside him. 'What is it?', she asks 60
as he brings hands thumb to thumb across his chest,
  as if to lift some large weight from his body.
'What is it, Ben', she asks again. But the heart once first
  to love others is now last to love itself,
and assurances of 'nothing, nothing' are glossed by memories 65
  of such passing pain on the rock road through Abercrombie.
Yet woman's eye side on to eyes reveals a sort
  of alabaster that has lost interest in light.
'Are you sure?' She asks. He is, he is, and so night resumes
  its difference from day, and they from it. 70
And then again the weight, in full, that Phyllis thinks
  'God, take him, quickly, and minimise the pain!'
until the enormity of the thought is realised,
  and the wish immediately reversed.
'Don't go', she cries, 'don't go' and urgency impresses 75
  itself: 'I don't fear death' he says, briefly
lucid, and remembering something read when still a boy,
  'it's the form death takes I'm afraid of, and of this I'm afraid.
Call the ambulance.' Outside and later, a friend
  is heard to ask a priest 'did you get here on time?' 80
But the answer, as to so many of the casual questions of history,
  is consumed in the slam of car door, and unheard.

III — Light on the hill

In the year of his birth he couldn't have known his Bathurst
  had been declared a city; coincidence,
of course, but not their subsequent pride, willingly shared. 85
  First I sat in his chair in Busby Street.

Then I thought how far I'd come since sitting on
   that throne in the palace in Knossos.
This was real: I *felt* like a Prime Minister,
   and relevant; I already knew I was powerful.   90
But I couldn't find his grave until I realised
   that this part of the cemetery was on
a hill, that every hill has at least its top,
   with butterflies and light, or as in Bathurst,
also its antiphonal, and especially now,   95
   Magpie Larks, its Golden Finches, Magpies,
its Willy Wagtails dressed as ever for every occasion,
   and of course Galahs, bird-tag-oblivious
of the large procession up from the cathedral
   and gathering, now, around an open grave.   100
Obviously, there won't always be Another Woman,
   however discreet, as there was at my father's
funeral, but on this occasion she was there,
   crying for the ex-Prime Minister,
and for the man for whom she couldn't too-openly grieve.   105
   And when a nation grieves, that's too much to bear.

Ethics

I

'Ethics' are what you write about when, having
    made your own, and loud mistakes, you want
to persuade the young to keep the peace in your old age.
    They'll take no more notice of you than I
took of the Dialogues of Plato, or Cicero's   5
    laboured set-piece 'conversations', written
in retirement and for his old friend, Brutus.
    Six months later he'd murdered Caesar!
If relevance is not demonstrated, no one will take
    notice, either of your ethics, or you.   10
What's the point of academic distinction between
    'pleasure' and 'absence of pain' except
to followers of 'Egoistic' and 'Universal Hedonism'?
    Or of arguments about 'innate' or 'learned'
conscience between 'Intuitionists' and 'Empiricists'?   15
    Or, concerning religious absolutes,
between metaphysical 'Rationalists' and the obscure
    'Categorical Imperative' of Kant?

II

Moral distinction between 'good' and 'bad'; aesthetic
    distinction between 'beautiful' and 'ugly',   20
will rarely interest the sunlight-normal Australian boy.
    There's only one thing on *his* mind
if the sun is out, even in Melbourne, and the magpies swagger,
    wings in pockets, among the daisies with their

head-bob to the wind and the random drop of bees; 25
    her thought, and feeling, will often be the same.
'And grass to our waists ... among she-oak, gum and wattle',
    John Batman said, of perhaps the same expanse,
'blocks' he'd 'purchased' from Wurundjeri Aborigines.
    'The deed signed by eight chiefs, each 30
handing me a portion of the soil ... full possession ...'
    As ethics, John Batman could have asked himself:

> *Do they realise I take this land*
> *to plough and sow and reap my fill forever?*
> *That I can no more guarantee* 35
> *my promised additional annual rent*
> *than fly my boat 'Rebecca' back to Launceston.*
> *That here they will never sing again or dance,*
> *or having danced, hunt and eat,*
> *or having eaten, sleep and dream?* 40
> *That any reasonable man among my people*
> *would say 600,000 acres was unfairly cheaply bought*
> *for these few blankets, knives, scissors, beads and flour?*

One knowing negative admits European deceit.
    Equally, any eight elders, of themselves or each other: 45

> *Does he realise this is only tribute he is paying?*
> *That we can no more 'sell' this land*
> *than fly with the Gang Gang and Galah*
> *that daily break the morning like a branch?*
> *That while we live we fire this earth to sky* 50
> *that in return sends rain, new grass*
> *and kangaroo to feed themselves, and us?*
> *That any reasonable man among our tribe*
> *would say that being on this land*

> *between the creek and hills for just one year* 55
> *was unfairly dearly sold*
> *for all those blankets, knives, scissors, beads and flour?*

One knowing negative admits Aboriginal deceit.

III

As if it needed him, still Batman gave his name
    to a nearby creek, otherwise already flowing. 60
Two days on, he'd found 'the place for the future village',
    then and now still a good description
of Melbourne, and the reluctance of much initial arrival.
    Then, the water was 'fresh and very deep',
the shore a store of banksia, she-oak, acacia 65
    and such eucalypts as enclose
an afternoon for a correct resonance of swans
    and the whirl of brown and white that is Stubble Quail;
that lands a Pelican in a long white wash, and settles
    Teal into a sunset beautiful and good. 70

IV

Now, oil rainbows the surface of the Yarra,
    and rubbish rots coloured and intricate
design against a much more modern watercolour:
    Effluent Brown, and that smell of civilisation
which, considered too closely, intensely questions the stomach. 75
    However bad, the sight is beautiful.

These streets forget their name every other kilometre,
    so that navigation is still an expertise
of tribal elders who walk a white suburban dreaming
    down lanes of brick and bitumen marked   80
by the lift and drop of dogs, and paling fences sema-
    phoring maintenance needs to a chemical moon.
Ugly, however good the food inside these best
    of city restaurants; and not even that, bad.

V

From an 'Ethics', then, of a universal Melbourne,   85
    it's possible to be beautiful and good,
beautiful and bad, or not beautiful and either,
    depending on how you depend upon yourself.

Fire

Winter is a country that visits, carrying rains
    that unwrap days inside at writing desks,
and evenings snug in leather chairs, with coffee, Conder
    and McCubbin prints, and gas-fire conversation
late about biographies, Australians dead,   5
    and travel to the city when we knew them.
Autumn tried to dress and then undress these un-
    deciduous landscapes, but I took little notice.
Summer I've more confidence about and love it,
    here, as a canvas of leucoxylon,   10
Salvation Jane, and parrots upside down in flowering
    gums, the slow smoke of beehives in
the Mt Lofty Ranges. Smoke is hard to paint in oils,
    even if you know that anyone
who truly sees can truly paint: glaze your smoke   15
    with a quick two flicks of brush and wrist, as in
my friend's canvas, where it smudges her valley like
    a seminal cloud of cloud and the day is
a lazy wading of cicadas in high grass
    that tinders itself, and the air, dry brown.   20
Closer up, use Cadmium Yellow for the flames,
    preferably with a number six camel hair
brush to lick the foreground of the canvas as flames
    are said to lick at growth from last year's rains.
In fact, left to themselves, flames greedily devour: 25
    'Grab the cat, your wallet, papers and car keys:
there's a bloody big bushfire coming up the gully.'
    Warning more than half serious is us-
ually vernacular, the basis of oath and art.
    Yet still this disbelief that something incap-   30
able of existence by itself, can travel so fast,
    can spit and crackle in undergrowth, then roar
like a jet, exploding trees and houses, with people

abused to leave with their lives. Safely out,
still she saw the panic-crashed cars, and corpses of those
   who foolishly ran, or who foolishly stayed.
Cattle burn where they stand, and sheep blacken
   into puppets, walking as if on stilts.
Wind is burning with audible agony, and flames,
   already twice the height of the trees, leap higher,
firing a flock of birds from the sky like a shower of fireworks.
   Nothing is spared except which the fires, scouting
ahead in hundred metre spots, inexplicably
   chose to ignore, leaping now this paddock
of flammable life to fire-ball here bare ground itself.
   Volunteers can only douse embers piling
on embers, and think later of irony piling on irony:
   that this truly was Ash Wednesday;
that the artist's studio with the painting of a fire was destroyed
   along with the canvas; that home, the volunteer,
his house destroyed, volunteered again, not knowing the fires
   a negligence of the power authority, his employer.
Other ironies are lost in months of recrimination,
   enquiries and reports on fragmented authority,
housing design, building regulation, fire
   prevention and communication procedures:
the basics always left till last, but needed first.
   This 'till September the following year, her house
rebuilt and for my stay. 'Spring is like a visit
   to the country', she said, 'except that you don't
need to go anywhere.' And then, touching the green
   that grew from the black, 'look at these epicormic
shoots: they have the intensity of flags at a festival.'
   And in her eye I could see a composition
of Banksia, Hakea, Eucalypt and sky, done with new brushes,
   and oils unopened now for many weeks.

Green

I love Brown Mountain and the Woolly Pomaderris,
    broad-petalled its yellow flowers above
Long-leaf Lomatia, leaf edges toothed like a bow-saw,
    but harmless among glabrous Mountain Pepper,
itself hotter to the taste than any Thai curry.   5
    And Sweet Bursaria, lustrous with black fruit,
if unforgiving in its thorny, star-flower fragility.
    Nearby is Rough Coprosma, druping an indigenous
red-orange, and Hickory and Sallow Wattles rioting
    national colours like a sporting team in victory.   10
And this what little I know without looking up — above
    are trees which without effort obtain respect
from anyone who has him- or herself been respected:
    The White Ash, *Eucalyptus fraxinoides,*
up like arms from shirts now basal stockings, scribbles   15
    like new tattoos in creamy-white bark of trunks
that hold, heady, the blue and green of sky on leaf.
    Proudly associated is Brown Barrel,
Eucalyptus fastigata, while behind on a ridge
    small crowned but crowning all, some Silvertop Ash   20
remind me of winter afternoons with Braidwood friends
    of honey thick on buttered bread, coffee,
and heat to open hands that 'stop' the pot-belly stove.
    We can know now such plants as we become:
think first of nature as God's imagination.   25
    Then, putting God aside (it is his fate),
think now of yourself as nature's imagination.
    'Consider' it says, 'keeping these, our colours
and forget how you'd differ from what you might have been.
    If old enough to have been, or not be, that,   30
can you identify for me what grows around you?

Is it itself and green, or coloured else?
If green, respect it: many men, timbercutters
   all, died for greed of a glabrous green,
a green that is now forgiveness above an ancient grave.'   35
   My luck would be to grow again, and as
Grevillea — *rosmarinifolia* so like, and liked by, me:
   sensitive and fast growing, if prickly,
but frost-tolerant and evergreen about Monaro.
   Sun-loving, this is loved by Honeyeaters   40
which, attempting heaven on the edge of the air, drink
   this nectar, song of my rich red spider-flowers.

Happiness

I could no more define happiness, Jenny, than fly.
    Whatever I think to suggest, exceptions quickly
leap to mind, proving that, as happiness, wrong.
    It is as nothing which gives me pleasure: good food
sustains, but is remembered as much for wine and conversation.   5
    Yet these demand more of themselves, and so,
even in moderation, can't be happiness either.
    I sometimes think we have it, or that it has us,
but then travel as if to look, or at least find something
    which ends in itself and half promises to stay.   10
But no travel, even here, is happiness for long:
    it must stop to be useful, and is so no longer travel.
Or it ends in a picnic on a panorama,
    arranged on a visit to the coast, north or south,
depending on where you don't live but think you might.   15
    Remember Wollongong, and our stop in Stanwell Park?
We sat on the Bald Hill, near where Lawrence Hargrave
    and James Swain assembled those box-kites and,
anchoring rope to a beach, linked a world to an idea.
    Then the thought, briefly entertained,   20
to each shake hands (as if kites wait when favoured with wind!)
    Quickly Hargrave stepped into the sling
he'd strapped beneath as one by one four box kites grip,
    the sling and Hargrave rise, with wind enough
to shout him its support, and agree him his ambition.   25
    We all know how he flew, umbilical
five metres to the world, himself mother to himself
    and his invention, but imagine his experience
of that wind, rather than the wind itself.
    And of the view, south to Lake Illawarra,   30
and back again: who hasn't stopped the car for it?

And imagine his thoughts on coming down, rather
than the coming down, first Swain then both pulling
   the lines and shouting, as much for joy as to
affirm themselves to each other and the day;   35
   then hurried packing, congratulations and kites
together: 'Whatever happens to me now, I can never be unhappy
   for very long. I've discovered, I am, myself
and my significance: because of these box-kites, we'll fly,
   here, over Wollongong, and around the world.'   40

Imagination

Jenny was adamant: 'Fancy; pure fancy. A slur on
    a Governor's name. Bligh was an officer;
can you really imagine him, on his knees, under a bed?'
    We were arguing about a watercolour, fancy,
or propaganda which showed a Governor coward to a coup.   5
    No defence to argue 'myth', that as
with Burke and Wills who, later, would never return,
    or Nellie Melba who, later still, would never
retire, because so many people *knew*, or
    imagined it thus, then so it had to be.   10
I could not appeal to public imagination to prove
    that same imagination to the public.
'Suppose', I said, 'we are all of us correct', always
    a good assumption. 'But how?' she asked.
'Imagine,' I added, taking us back to 1808   15
    and a very different Australia Day.
'Imagine what we know to be true', I said, forgetting
    myself in order to remember everything else.
'"Lieutenant-Governor" Johnston leads four hundred troop
    of New South Wales Corps, regimental colours   20
streaming out of Bligh Street into afternoon sun;
    a band approximates The *British Grenadiers,*
while curious Sydney citizens for whom this history
    is ostensibly being made, run along behind.
These soldiers swarm swear and noise themselves throughout   25
    the Government House; a woman is arrested.
"Come with me", a trooper orders, or perhaps half
    observes and, unaware of the parody
and without looking back, leads a lady down some stairs.
    "Mary Putland, Sir", he says, presenting   30
or delivering to Major Johnston. "The Governor's Daughter."

Her tongue confirms her, and her father's, name.
More "damn his eyes" and "search again" continue down,
    while up, along and back, in a small end room,
the Governor secretes or destroys exhibits for a trial.   35
    His vest so stuffed with the papers he must hold,
he has just one hand left to find the note that damns
    The Perturbator, and justifies himself.
"That's it", he shouts and lunges for a document
    which drops, as paper will: first left then right,   40
or north and south: up and down and under the bed.
    The Governor drops and crawls: it would be over,
against the wall, which he reaches, leaving his feet
    for the soldier who heard him to see, and pull.
So, though probably under part of the bed, he wasn't   45
    necessarily hiding', I concluded.
Jenny had to agree. Then, eyeing me facetiously,
    'I suppose you also know what was on
that piece of paper?' But now I grinned, and hugely. 'No;'
    I said, *'that* would be pure fancy.'   50

Jenny

The Wedge-tailed Eagle doesn't wonder why that Magpies
    Currawongs and Crows don't fly so high;
rather, he gets on with his soaring, riding the thermals
    over Toolbrunup and the Stirling Range,
whose rows of gigantic if long-worn molars,   5
    that take the tongue of plains beyond Albany
to a far sky of mouth in cloud-lined throat.
    His eyes are skinned for prey he can take to nest,
or he is up and high for a sheer joy of flying.
    I too soar in my way, for when   10
a poet like me has a woman like you and country like
    Australia, how can I fail a lasting interest?
How can I not echo in the minds of all the song, or lament,
    which outlives any children we could produce?

Kenosis

A decade since his death, and still it's possible
    to kick his coins from sand on Galilee:
Augustus obverse to himself as God, hero or man.
    I walked there once, myself the second of three;
the third an immanence bestowing eminence,   5
    on me or, for joy of the first, my father.
He now is where he will always be, so I guess
    his answer to a question for which truth is always
too obvious: 'Can anything good come out of Naz-
    areth?' Or Capernaum, or Cabramatta?   10
Sisters, suburbs; brothers, towns — all agree:
    why separate as deity what must
be given up to be as man again? Prophet
    and poet both lack honour of place and time:
either observing children as substitute, un-   15
    achieved selves, or stressing feeling as guide
to thought in whatever life there is in life to come.
    We may well be another attempt at ourselves:
whether 'having children', or 'making a sacrifice'
    believing at least our work to be divine.   20
But any choice is sacrifice and kenosis;
    all children never had, having tried,
a grieving that passes. I tell you it is a divinity
    to be alive, however briefly. Look:
already you are my heirs, sharing this past that crowds   25
    behind us in the mirror, demanding to be
part of the image you take when you go, glad to give up
    some of this life for the sake of son or daughter
as I give up the possibility of either
    for the possibility of you.   30
Truly, our future is behind us; this history we live

    is a present, constantly renewed,
an immortality of endless tomorrows independent
    of death, that says 'because I am read in myself,
I am forever in my thought and the thought of all: 35
    so I live forever by being me.'
We pour our self to other selves as ideas imagined
    on ideas perpetuate themselves in mind,
and civilisation; as the Murrumbidgee, in ignorance
    of itself and years of high mountains,   40
flows again for limestone needing to be smooth rock;
    for casuarina needing to be green tree;
for the river bends that need to meander towards sky
    and clouds, themselves needing river to be seen in.
To be immortal is not always to be known: I had a daughter   45
    once who died before she was never born.

Letter (an appeal)

You, my few friends, those of you not still aching
    for Europe and calling the pain 'multiculturalism',
whether you're now someone else, or your own happy selves:
    to you I raise this glass of Coonawarra Red.
It was made almost in the extended shadow of that mountain   5
    that cups the Blue Lake, where Adam Lindsay
Gordon spurred his horse to leap higher and longer
    than he was ever able to scan himself.
Pity. You know better, so to you I want to put
    a question, wiping from my face this cold   10
white wine that is the mist and rain of Penola:
    tell me, as you would were I an auditor,
chairman of a Select Committee of the Senate,
    or a priest administering last rites; tell me
whether you really think that this country is your home?   15
    Whether this continent, which slowly
edges north, painfully towing Tasmania
    as a woodchipped haemorrhoid, actually
contains even one hectare which agrees with you?
    I'm writing to you 'pre-Greenhouse'; not to frighten,   20
or admonish (we are, after all, ourselves and pretended
    European in our fate) but to say
I no longer look in the mirror because the buffalo,
    cane toads, camels, carp, cats, dogs,
donkeys, foxes, goats, horses, pigs and rabbits   25
    that I see there are so ugly.
They make such noisy noise I've turned the radio off.
    Their habits are so filthy I no longer read the papers.
And yet, because from the top of Toolbrunup I've seen
    a Wedge-tailed Eagle fly just beneath me,   30
I know that just one bird can lift a landscape into

my mouth as one loud gasp, giving air
enough to defend a continent with words of hope.
   This, perhaps, I can do by naming things,
so let me abbreviate, and say greater and lesser,
   eastern and western, central and short-tailed,
hair-footed and hairy-nosed, rufous, brush-tailed,
   stick-nest, and dusky-hoping: bandicoot,
bat, bettong, bilby, dunnart, kangaroo, kowari,
   kultarr, mouse, mulgara, numbat, phascogale,
possum, potoroo, quoll, rat, wallaby and wombat.
   There's a mouth full of extinction and near
extinction you can also name, and loudly — but beware:
   even emptiness can be 'addressed' by bureaucracy.
Meanwhile, have you noticed how, the faster we pour the salt
   on food, the faster it surfaces in the Murray Basin
as adolescent pustules that get worse, and not better, with age?
   How summer and winter are experienced more and more
as inconvenient inversions of each other, and not
   as their relatively hot and cold selves,
which, respectively, used to ripen over our heads like fruit,
   or recede into the earth at our approach?
How continually we invade ourselves and call it 'immigration'?
   How more and more we want to believe,
and in anything, even when we know we can't?
   Then I drink to you and an understanding
of this end of a century which consumed the bush
   I used to walk in, singing loudly in
my boy-scout uniform and ironically ignorant
   royal plural 'we're here because we're here',
and say 'Here's to you; if you make it into the next
   century, and you're still able to live
above the ground, keep your head down: extinction
   is forever, black and white and always.'

Because I have no job or purpose other than 65
    to be myself, and because no one with
a job or purpose will be believed, I can affirm
    that this Monaro, high and generous,
that this south-east, populated and also gen-
    erous, that in fact this continent, 70
large, beautiful, naive and generous,
    was once the best place in the world
to be undecided about the meaning of the life
    of everything other than ourselves.
Do say something, or write within the next twelve months. 75
    I'd like to think you think of things that made me
important to myself, and thus to you — as
    it is, I'm no longer certain whether
I'm sincerely, or just faithfully, yours (the date
    is 24th of next month, last year). 80

Manly

Avalon has its fine white sand, Bondi Beach its tourists,
    and Cronulla its shells if you know where to look.
But in Sydney's alphabet of beaches, Manly is centrepiece,
    and rightly. If you wrote home about it, you were brief
('join me'); if you read about it, you came, across the harbour   5
    and that swell through the Heads, in ferries whose names began
with 'B' or 'K', and carried the inevitable smart alecs
    who leapt off well before the boat was moored.
The boys who dived for pennies near the pier were more-sensibly
    brave, and surfaced with a coin in their teeth   10
and a glint in their eye, as if they'd dared and beaten a diff-
    erent, less-forgiving, ferryman.
When a whale came ashore in 1790, word was sent
    to other tribes, to come and share the blubber:
Manly was 'manly' then and not just because Governor   15
    Phillip thought Aborigines dignified;
'womanly', obviously, they were as well.   Personally,
    I love the place, and whether, aged eight, with a cloud
of fairy-floss in my hand, or thirty-eight,
    with a piece of fish shaped like a scale-model surfboard,   20
and forgetting, because of the jazz on The Corso, that vinegar
    had soaked the chips as sea soaks the sand
and these little bits of Norfolk Pine between
    my toes, it, Manly, has loved me.
Not even the cymbals of the Salvos could drown-out those waves   25
    that shout each other down upon the shore.
And late in the afternoon, wet sand still glitters like so many
    mirrors, illuminating these memories, and years.
Every Australian I know has swum here, intends to,
    or would have, in another day or life in Manly.   30

Nouns and colonial verbs

Transitional or transitive all relationships,
    like nouns and colonial verbs. Like Cabramatta,
'place of the Cobra grub', and me, pretend-aristocrat
    of mud castles in my childhood backyard.
Or afternoon bicycle rides to the George's river to swim,   5
    raid vineyards and generally boy the world
that mothers clean up, thankless, afterwards. Mine raised,
    or hoped, five children with dad away on ships.
He, like John Macarthur, could never quite believe
    a woman's world near Liverpool, or beyond   10
at Camden, once 'The Cowpastures', of our excursions,
    where Elizabeth Macarthur also lived
a husband's absence on the ships, if of another age.
    Her days' nights now years of verbs and nouns:
'Separate wethers, divide ewes into flocks of three hundred;   15
    add the rams, four to six, when breeding.
Ensure each flock has an attendant and attentive, shepherd.
    Instruct each one: "out at dawn, back
by night, beware of poachers, dingoes, flood or fire."
    Rebuild the shepherds' huts destroyed by Natives.   20
Replace the shepherds speared by same; pray against drought.
    Wash merinos, before shearing, at Elizabeth Farm.
Shear, and with the classer. Export the fine merino,
    send the coarse to the female factory.
Dairy the cows; farm pigs, barley, oats and wheat ...   25
    Verb I am to these convicts, servants and children.
Garden the vegetables, preserve today, jam tomorrow.
    Orchard almonds, apricots peaches and pears ...'
I interrupt: a woman's work is ever done
    this way — in full and competent alone;   30
but less if home a man has house. And so my mother.
    Her father farmed his horizons of sheep at 'Myall',
on Urangeline, where once I worked as rouseabout,

    shore a sheep with blades, and thought of Jackie Howe
eponymously clad in himself, and moleskins,   35
    eyeing the drafting yards on Alice Downs:
'Lambs the lot, and if almost hoggets, few dags or snaggers,'
    he thought; 'today's the day for a run on a record.'
The shed, aware, ensures the catching pen's kept full,
    the fleeces thrown to table, locks swept aside   40
before the next is shoulder-carried, legs tabled-out,
    to be shorn from the ghost of a would-be self then pushed
head-first and hooves teeth-screeching, down galvanised chute
    to counting yard now full to disbelieving.
Bets have been placed; so money will be won and lost.   45
    An edge, blunt but felt, is on the banter:
'You've done enough man! You've done enough!' a shearer shouts,
    as tally nears three hundred: one tickles his ribs,
one jumps on his back, another returns his lamb to the pen.
    Yet again he changes blades, considers the total: 50
three hundred and twenty one and twenty minutes in hand
    along with a record: 'I can afford to stop;
then the talk will also be of what I could have done.
    The number's set — no need to limit the legend.'

I put the blades down with respect. When you have,   55
    approximate, the heart of a hero's life,
heard the wisdom that condenses to the effortless aside
    tutored by a long and well-lived life,
then home you watch a winter sunset with a different eye:
    clouds may attempt colours in their final wool,   60
and winds a matching art-work on the surface of a lake;
    but now you think or imagine yourself imagine:
'I know what I'm doing and what, with determination,
    can be achieved; I don't need adjectives.'

Other

Other is everything: opportunity, threat,
  location and dislocation, dichotomy and
alternatives that, being everyone else, are eventually us.
  'Any other questions?' asked the chairman,
this time in the Royal Hotel, packed to hear 5
  others, and Dan Deniehy: 'If here
the common water mole becomes the Duck-Billed Platy-
  pus, must we accept degenerate English
favour of this bunyip aristocracy?'
  Ignore the slur on our fauna: at such 10
a speech crowds roar the Affirmative 'No', that non-
  negotiable vowel formed on the tongue, and flung
from the lips when privilege in Australia is proposed.
  In other words, they agreed, and jugs
of porter, black from weeks of mashed wort hops, wobbled 15
  on other tables, and spilled on this one where,
it seems, I am always sitting. Had I been anxious
  to speak or ask a question, my heart would
have pounded like the heavy hammers in a gold stamper,
  until someone in the audience revealed, 20
as it were, my 'vein' of concern. Were I,
  on the other hand, sitting in
the 'other place', I'd be in a Parliament,
  where one House thus describes, if two, the other:
'Point of order, Madame Speaker, the debate is now 25
  on other matters.' *Howls of derision
from the other side,* as Hansard might have annotated,
  missing backbench comment about a Member
for Maranoa's origins on the other side of the blanket.
  'Sit down; there's no point of order.' 30
A most-feared threat is still the 'other woman' (notice

it's never the 'other man', however the adulterous
triangle may be constructed). *She* always threatens
respectable marriages, suggesting that
something other than duty may sensibly govern good life; 35
he simply has something 'on the side'.
But the 'other half' always live and love differently:
either because they live on the other side
of tracks that snake a train, diesel and tall, through towns
like Cairns, or because they live and love at all. 40

Poetry

It's like love: you know how you don't know, and then
    it's too late because you've said something?
Or you do know, being a little older, and write yourself
    in or out of it, becoming a poet
in the process: no wonder the one celebrates the other!   5
    In neither can there be deceit, hard heart-
edness and lack of ambition; these never won a woman,
    or obtained that license to receive, unannounced,
those whom we still choose to call 'the Muses'.
    You can't govern with poetry, and yet without it,   10
a nation is not worth governing, or ungovernable.
    If it sells, it's not thought good, though
it may be; if it doesn't, it is, though we may know it's not.
    You can't use it for propaganda, to preach,
or convey information: though fact, in fact and end-   15
    lessly updated, is mere and continuous fiction,
while a poem, as fiction, can yet become a timeless fact.
    'So you're writing a book, Tim?' my aunt
from Wentworthville once asked. 'A novel, is it?' 'No;'
    I said, 'a book of poems', and her eyes   20
dropped with their message to the floor: poetry equals
    adolescence; novels maturity.
God, but it seems no aunt was ever told that the best
    novelists are poets who simply decided
to be verbose, and restrict their appeal to present   25
    generations, where the money is.
And so we call a poetry useless, irrelevant;
    a luxury first to go when 'times are tough'.
But aren't they always? And isn't it always the 'always' of poetry
    we demand at birth, death and commitments which,   30
like marriage and departures of all kinds, create the other
    births and deaths that are, or pass for, life?

Quadrilles

1 — The Collingwood Tote

Now John Wren didn't drink or smoke,
was, some would say, a spiv, too;
but the kind of bloke
if you went to, broke,
he'd have a pound to give you.   5

'My teashop? No!' he'd quietly gloat:
'I earned that pound from horses,
from the starting-price quote
of my Collingwood Tote
on several likely courses.'   10

And though several likely raids were staged
upon his toting teashop,
inside the cage
not a single page
of tickets did they see drop.   15

So on Cup Day morn, the Law, with force,
sat police in occupation;
they backed, of course,
not a single horse,
on this race-day of a nation.   20

No punters lined the Tote's laneways,
you bet they thought it funny,
for to pass the days
police talked of ways
of playing cards, for money.   25

— *The heads of the people* (7 August 1847)

2 — The flying pieman

'Pies! Hot pies!' shouted William King.
'Pork, mutton: come and buy, man!
For the sweetest thing
try the apple fling:
from your Friendly Flying Pieman!'   5

'Or kidney pie by the Sydney sea,
with gravy, on a platter,
then embark with tea
from the Circular Quay,
and steam to Parramatta.'   10

And steam they did, nor spare the spray,
and found ... "I'll testify, man:
he'd run all the way
and with his tray;
it was the Flying Pieman!   15

"Again he sold them, fruit and meats,
we ate them all with pleasure,
and believed his feats
in the Sydney streets
for no man's had his measure."   20

Congested now, that road would baulk
both motorist and pieman;
to run or walk
don't even talk;
no way you'd even try, man.   25

— *The Bulletin* (10 December 1892)

3 — The Speaker's Mace

Now girls, please take your place:
I declare this House 'in order'.
With bows of lace,
this Speaker's Mace
makes madame also warder.   5

Today we have the case
of the IOU for Mary:
to accept with grace,
perhaps give chase,
or in future be more chary.   10

'This Note is no disgrace:
he is my Local Member;
I know his face,
if needs could trace,
should he fail me come November.'   15

"Our life leaves little space
for charity advances;
to take the pace
up that staircase
for cash I take my chances."   20

Resolved now in this Place,
On Boccaccio's the onus:
we melt the Mace
for the silver base
and vote ourselves a bonus.   25

Requiem

First, for my mother, Olive Emma, and then for anyone [A,B]

Because I read you this, so you will follow
and pick up left or right and as I say,
and throw down left or right and as I say,
hand for hand, mind for mind and soul for soul.

We are [A,B] as [A,B] was us,   5
and, like [him or her] come from this life,
through earth and water, air
and the spaces they inhabit.

First and left, we pick this up,
earth and water, air,   10
elements to which you return,
and another life for others and for us.

If we didn't touch before,
then with what we hold we touch now,
though you die before your breath stop,   15
with it, or later in our forgetfulness.

Second and right, we pick this up,
earth and water, air,
elements to which we return,
and another life for others and for us.   20

If we didn't speak before,
we speak now,
though you die before your breath stop,
with it, or later in our forgetfulness.

Because I read you this, we will remember, 25
and give to land, sea or space of sky
once and left to now let go,
again and right to say "Goodbye".

Saturday

Coffee doubles up, or goes to tea with milk.
    So breakfast extends, as do the papers, fat
on today, with tomorrow equally black and white and certain.
    (The past is always a colour supplement).
The week becomes itself and the chores that are the house: 5
    The washing of days dirtied in our clothes;
the odd jobs with the even chance of being done;
    the shopping for food or film, or play or music:
demands described as 'life', itself something else.
    This past is bleaching, the colour of forgetfullness, 10
and futures easily black if feelings are allowed;
    colour I give to this present and yours,
and tax-returns that attempt to explain how it's possible
    to have so little money, while being so well known.

Tradition

I sing in C the tactics of the tenor clef:
    Toby Tosspot and the plate tectonics of being
a sober Prime Minister; the teacher who tipped-off
    that train; Tasmania's tortuous trilogy
of rivers, dams and trees: this is our tradition.   5
    As it was handed to me, so I hand it
on to you, noting the lore with the letter.
    To and fro, to and fro: Sturt
went blind, as Burke and Wills would testify, traipsing
    to the tragedy that used to be and still is   10
the outback, now a traveller's tale of Tamarisk trees,
    feral ferals on any number of legs
ours included, and salt, payback for a religion
    that would traduce, transfix, transfer and transpose.
Let me say that I too would have stopped that train,   15
    and saved those police. So would have you: topers
travellers or top-enders, whether rich enough
    to live in topography, or,
like us, in town. You may talk or write to someone
    who will laugh, cry or promise (but rarely carry out)   20
revenge, passing on the general thrust of things:
    who it was who got the Court House cleaned;
the way that tourists pose in front of steamed sandstone;
    the tennis tournaments we used to win, and
without trying, on TV sets inside where,   25
    more usually, there is the handing down of statements,
examination of beliefs — legends and customs, even —
    with which one generation continues to
convince, or convict another, the one allowing
    imagination a role in our happiness,   30
the other maintaining as the present a kind of brutalised
    past, with overseer, cat in hand
and sickening grin, removing convicts, pair by pair,
    from twenty holding a whole cedar log on their shoulders.

Unless

Unless, until, if then/else: these are the conditions
    I'm imposing because I have no options.
It might be thought that I am free, since I can choose
    to be myself while you must approximate
yourself to a job, a day and your wages' concept of you.   5
    Admit it: a friend once told you 'The best poet
is the one that costs me nothing' — and you agreed,
    unaware of where he'd picked up the pentameter.
Listen more closely next time: everything of interest
    may already have been scanned by someone   10
who, like my mother, had long been taken for granted.
    What do you think otherwise happens to words?
Yours and mine are important because, when governments
    finally legislate all fiction as plausible fact,
and corporations become their price points and their products,   15
    your thought, and this, will be all we have.
Don't blame me if, through lack of interest, the future
    becomes an eternal present, contemptuously
uncontemplated — for well you know that no one else
    will bother to say what you might be capable of feeling.   20
So, and unless you can afford not to be yourself:
    buy this book while I live. I need the money.

Vegemite

Morning. The rattle of cereal and pour of milk. Coffee
    with, over imaginative newspaper speculation
on other newspaper speculation, toast and Vegemite:
    breakfast wouldn't be my country without it.
But first, a swim with my brother-in-law at Avalon   5
    Beach: the seagulls bodysurfing above,
us below, as when young you find yourself
    those waves that carry you and lips kiss-up
to the shore, sand and water in your hair, hands out,
    palms down, edge of continent between   10
fingers and thumbs, horizon draining to your toes.
    Ah! To then stand upon it and think:
breakfast! Now my hair spumes with soap on my head,
    and the shower rose roars its seagulls at
my sea-salted skin. Dry, I apply myself   15
    to my toast, and yes: butter is spuming
at the edge of the knife, and another argument of seagulls
    flocks for the set-square corners that leave my plate
its Poisson distribution of breadcrumbs, a passable
    imitation of sand. Memories   20
that don't involve food, and people eating it,
    will always starve on the page, or if in the mouth,
trail into years of 'who can say how it really was?'
    and disappointment in the eyes of nephews and nieces.

Women

'Take it back', said Caroline Chisholm, rejecting the dray
    when her first group of immigrants refused
to go bush; 'but bring me two as good tomorrow morning.'
    I learned Australia from such women, and settlers
who, knowing no better, made themselves the better to know.   5
    Determination was thirty immigrants to ride
and walk: fifteen up, fifteen down, and turn-
    about every other mile, bridge or hill.
Parramatta Road was a bush track then, past Grose's Farm,
    the new Racecourse, and Robert Johnston's 'Annandale':   10
family and familiar certainties to one generation,
    and travellers for the Counties and beyond.
'More Catholic Irish immigrants for this Protestant English
    colony, Mrs Chisholm?' Some prejudice
there is that won't be edited by the anapaestic   15
    rhythm of horses hooves, the stilling heat
of late November sun, the coloured flash of Rainbow
    Lorikeet, or anything made by
a nineteenth century God west of the Great Divide.
    'Nothing personal,' he said; 'nothing personal.'   20
But with John Dunmore Lang, everything was personal,
    each day a conspiracy against the last
and perhaps the next. Still, she could forgive him himself.
    Others would go to Goulburn whence he'd come,
where rain is so heavy it seems to bring down the gravity   25
    with it and men sink to their knees, bullocks to
their bellies, and wagons to their axles in High Street mud;
    where sun-bleached skeletons swing about
the prison yard like forgotten washing, visible
    to shoppers of soap, English novels and best   30
porter at Solomon and Levy, or Benjamin and Moses.
    They shut those shops all day that day that Mary
Ann Brownlow died; rejecting 'the love that knows of nothing

left to love', she, instead, loved all,
and demonstrably, even as they prepared the scaffold
   on which she was to trip, apologising
to a priest more in need of grace than she.
   They love us, and we kill them. Caroline Chisholm
went to Yass, and I, in my other century,
   to Canberra where, writing myself a guide
to a capital of a continent, I visited
   the cemetery at St John's, Canberry.
Church records would deny that Mary Ann is buried here,
   but I have it from Stuart collateral
to Hamilton Hume that she is. They also say
   the first tune played on the organ was 'Rory O'More',
to which several girls danced up and down the aisle:
   joy is still the highest respect, and as eagerly
paid as accepted. Now I look from the grave to a uniformed noise
   of schoolgirls emerging from the church and running
with themselves like spring lambs, marvelling that they live,
   can jump, fall, rise and run again.
Here, one shouting loudly to her friend reminds me
   of Judith Anderson, on a beach, somewhere,
and shouting her lines above the sound of the waves as voice-
   production for that other coastline: the footlights
in a theatre. Here, with a pack on her back,
   perhaps another Marie Byles, Bush-
walker to the Himalayas and example-
   alphabet of women-possibilities.
And there, oh there, the daughter I never had, skipping
   as I imagine daughters are supposed to skip:
arms flapping along with those of her class-room friend
   like Sulphur-crested Cockatoos grown
away from the nest and screeching their scrape of sandpaper
   on sandpaper, which, whenever I hear it,
still is sweeter than the most harmonious music,
   bowed blown or plucked by anybody.

X-Roads

I

It's a boy! And you're the first of readers to know.
    Resigned or reasoned acceptance of childlessness
now ends, as do most joys of self-expecting life:
    the silverplated breakfasts huge with coffee
in country pubs, the leisured look at drop-slab huts,   5
    Federation, or other architecture;
the bush and walking blue-green days of trees and birds
    most always new to sight, most still our own;
the nights subsequent in, perhaps, Carnavon Gorge
    if north, or camped upon The Coorong, south,   10
and all in winter wild with flowers. Home, more gas-fire
    conversation late, and fine red wine:
the searching out of self in identifiable scenery,
    and best of country enjoyed in best of life.

II

Thus far, then, you can imagine our imaginings,   15
    due January and for the rest of our lives,
another life for us, a baby and a son.
    We thought we wanted; had tried too hard for wanting.
Accepting this, deciding to be more like ourselves,
    we made ourselves the easier to resemble: 20
my self decided to love myself, though quite obliquely
    so as not to frighten, the better able
then to best love you, my heirs and heritage
    regardless of responsibility.
So taking myself at my numerous words, relaxing,   25
    accepting our acceptance as our fate,
I have as gift that miracle of life in life
    and the poet's only other inspiration.

III

John will first find us; later, with luck himself.
    'She'll bloom', the doctor says, eyes me to her. 30
And bloom she does, though nothing I've seen prepares me how:
    Skin is never like the eucalypt bark,
yet so the Candlebark attempts such sheen in season;
    nor eyes an eagerness of open flowers,
yet so the Daisy greets our sun in Woden days. 35
    Hair is hardly fine phyllode of wattle,
but still the wind accepts hers so, as show or presence.
    Thus Jenny blooms plurality as life,
the only miracle greater than love, and force more forceful;
    the only determination more hopeful than hope, 40
the only flower not a flower that blooms as flower:
    and the only thing in everything in the world.

IV

How much can you sensibly *tell* a teenage boy,
    or your country, and is there a difference?
Do you understate by power of example? 45
    Or do you say straight out 'Don't pretend
to be European; this Australia's your only chance.'?
    Even a nation of immigrants, living
in their heads and overseas, must come of age with age.
    I hope he never sees what I foresee: 50
cities at war within, and then between, themselves;
    the air become disease; life underground;
and government so desperate to be relevant
    that novelists and poets are asked to rule.
A poet agrees, but on one impossible condition: 55
    'Promise me', she says, 'that you'll be yourselves.'

V

Now I know the child is truly 'father to
    the man', and even before the child is born!
Will I be good enough to be good, as man and father?
    Can I become what you expect of me?   60
Can you, I of you? And he, indeed, of himself?
    Questions have a habit of asking themselves,
while answers can take a life of time and imagination
    and still beg all belief and understanding.
In time perhaps he'll enjoy what always gave me pleasure: 65
    the book that cannot be put down unread;
travel through what remains, if unaware what remains of what;
    conversation with friends, if friends remain;
the day that holds September sun to twenty degrees,
    and wind that lifts at dresses of beautiful women.   70

Yass

No one could tell me why but they said that Henry O'Brien
    didn't want brother Cornelius to sell
Cooma Cottage to Hamilton Hume; *he'd* come back
    to buy the history he'd made, going away:
"A later generation, Mr Hovel, will raise
    an obelisk on this campsite near Fish River."
It's not given to all of us to discover the country
    we're born in, but we can learn to love landscape.
It is always and only our face, the face of our nature.
    The grass our hair, skin another soil
from which to produce this or that crop, while others run
    or are run by, sheep, fine wool and bales of it.
I too grow here, skin and song to such eternal landscapes:
    the trip to market, and cattle penned for sale;
the son, single and mind-set to the week he'd met the eyes
    and then the girl who chipped him his careless remark.
"She must be interested: no one else'd be game."
    Another bidding proceeds per kilo in ten cent
steps and shouts 'till the rumps of cattle are anointed
    with paint to signify sale, and imminent death.
I'll skip that detail: let's just say that Yass can still
    arrange to accidentally meet those
who must be met, in Comur Street on Friday after-
    noons, or Saturday mornings, when everyone
relaxes, in order to be busier than ever.
    That they still marry in new St Augustine's
or old St Clement's depending on where the cross is worn
    and how it is described. If horses no longer
carry Father ('never-out-of-the-saddle') Therry
    around his Irish parish the size of England,
the miracle that is the birth of children remains

    as does the water that is sprinkled on
their heads and sparkles from acacias in gusts of wind
    and light near Yass River after rain.
We must go away before we can come back, and age   35
    before something complex, and then nothing complex,
can be seen in a simple backyard off Grampian Street,
    in a paddock beneath a Blakely's Red Gum (older
than any local can remember) or on a dirt
    track between two properties (now united)   40
where, in a stand of eucalypts marvellously untouched,
    a Sacred Kingfisher sits, blue, green, black
and holy-white on a branch in sky. He (for it is he)
    is clear in his eye as to who we are,
apparently interested in our own halcyon days   45
    and what we discovered when we went away.

Zeitgeist
Ille ego qui fuerim ...

My life so far

I

I was eldest of five: three sisters, a brother third youngest,
    and born in the Women's Hospital in Christopher
Brennan's Crown Street, 1943.
    Sydney, then, was full of hats, most men's
'Akubra', like mine when seven, sometimes tipped to women,   5
    often off indoors, and always for a national anthem
beseeching God to save yet another foreign monarch.
    If we thought ourselves British, *they* made no such mistake,
and used us with all the conscience of extravagant generals.
    War, meanwhile, contradicted the Pacific,   10
as did Jack Lang the Labor Party once too often.
    Streeton had died, knighted for his pictures,
and benighted by poverty, Shaw Neilson the year before:
    if a time to be born, then a time to quickly grow out of.

II

Life, I remember, began the day my father died: 15
    suddenly, much depended on my being me.
Later, I would travel to Greece, study the language
    and attempt to comprehend the man as myself.
Sure, when home from ships more travelled than any Argo,
    We'd run, brother and sisters, to the gate to greet him,   20
each of us hoping to be first lifted high, so huge and powerful,
    the shouting for turns, the dog an ostinato;
and sure, the trip one day to see him hired in Sydney
    and men nervous behind loud cigarettes:

'*Able Bodied Seaman for the Iron Flinders to Whyalla!*' 25
    and the sight of Dad, centre of the circle, approved:
obviously able to endlessly shovel coal to ships' boilers.
    I buried him in Newcastle, and went home ignorant.

III

Cabramatta, then, was my 'native place',
    though the national capital, Canberra, now is home. 30
School was school; nor need I catalogue universities:
    education is best from people, not courses.
Piano I studied with Freda Franks, composition
    with Peter Sculthorpe, art with Tom Bass,
and, when old enough to have something to write 35
    about, poetry with Judith Wright.
But first, like any man ignorant of his ignorance,
    though at least aware of that, I travelled:
Europe when it was relevant; Asia now that we are,
    the Americas and Russia; this continent complete. 40
The places you go to when you know you're going to go places,
    and the mothering place to which you always return.

IV

Many, they say, are the mothers of lyric poets; and many,
    the grandmothers, who cooked for Ned Kelly
at Younghusband's Station in 1879. 45
    But my mother disowned me, and her mother,
Browne with an 'e', couldn't even pronounce my name.
    Inevitable, then, that young I'd think myself 'Greek'.
Jenny, it was, who showed me how to grow like a eucalypt,
    but I didn't dream I'd wake with a nation, or for it! 50
I took up poetry to make something Australian

of myself; now, it's my joy to find
that I've also made something of Australian poetry.
    If, therefore, I'm hopeful for the future,
it's because, having written myself into it,   55
    I know it has to be there, and safe with you.

V

Large hands (a tenth with ease) gave me my grip on Beethoven
    (people paid to hear me play piano);
large feet, with skin like leather, served school in lieu of shoes
    (of course, I studied violin as well!).   60
If quick to temper and slow to forgive or forget, not malicious.
    Medium height, small-framed, almost thin,
crown-bald with a hair line that recedes with the tide of years,
    I'm told I look like anything but a poet.
But I live and write at the edge of myself and centre of my art,   65
    driven, like an organist in a fugue by Bach,
hands and feet tracing a complex counterpoint,
    to catch the cadence that will swell to Tierce de Picardie.
And holding the attention of all, some quite in spite of themselves,
    I end as player and all the music written.   70

VI

But first I had to work, both for myself and others:
    Clerk Railways, Clerk PMG,
then Clerk Departments of Trade, and Public Service Board.
    Those last promotions (the one to the capital, the other
while here) were all I ever had: I just couldn't pretend.   75
    Make that plain and you can't expect to be liked.
First my furlough, then other leave, then resignation:
    'I insist,' said Jenny, 'for both our sakes.'

Only then did I discover how much a job defines,
    and through its purpose, provides a self-esteem.   80
I didn't shout 'UNEMPLOYED at last!' I cried.
    Such my anger with such bureaucracy.
Thus fully-paid, I repossessed myself and life,
    and shared myself again among my trees.

VII

Yet I hadn't always allowed myself to love the bush;   85
    (children of my generation had been warned:
'trees that refuse to drop their leaves can't expect to be loved.')
    Such perversity I now ignore
and insist on enjoying this bush as much as it enjoys me.
    Look at this view from upon Gibraltar Rocks: 90
how the trees cloud the land as clouds tree the sky;
    how the rocks themselves are, and reach-up for,
a firmament. How below, beside and 'round about me
    the Hickory Wattle, Broad-leaved Peppermint,
Silver Banksia, Apple Box and Dogwood extend   95
    their pungent, powerful and entirely welcome, welcome.
This bush knows me as well as I know it, and loves
    accordingly; in time so might we all.

VIII

No one ever told us that no one would ever tell us,
    did they? That we'd have to decide what heroes we'd need,   100
who they'd be, and what they'd have done for themselves, and us.
    This I'm pleased to have begun to do.
I came late to poetry as to my marriage,
    determined to be certain and committed to both.
Proud of my Greek extraction, yet I live Australian,   105

    placing myself in tradition with 'our four':
Harpur, Kendall, Paterson and Wright (as well as Pindar)
    and pleased to be read by those who enjoy my pleasures.
The best, I've found, is often too obviously obvious;
    the worst, a comfort allowing little else.   110
So though I give myself direction, you can still choose
    (acknowledgement will not be necessary).

IX

Nine was my beginning and nine will be my end.
    (If I admit I was here before and again before that,
it's to accept that this is not the only universe;   115
    that the residual of these atoms is a kind of God.)
Your generation will never know what happened to us.
    Daily we waited for change, determined not to,
somehow hoping to discover why we had to drift north.
    Yearly we yearned for love, hated ourselves,   120
but always insisted on electing politicians with faces
    that reflected us like highly polished mirrors.
Yet on my shoulder sleeps my eight-day old son;
    in my head the concept of my next four books,
and beside me, Jenny, as well sleep-weary, but contemplating   125
    happiness such as we have never known.

Your life so far

I

Because I now know who I am, I can tell you
    who you are. Regardless of where you might
have been born, you are beginning to be Australian.
    You are beginning to get up in the morning   130
and marvel at sunrise which pastes the colour of wheat
    over a demonstrably edible landscape.
You are beginning to eat the landscape. You have been,
    on more than one occasion, mistaken for the landscape.
You are not taking offence; on the contrary,   135
    you are cancelling holidays overseas
because of your preference to succour and enjoy
    roots that grow regardless of rainfall patterns.
You are, in fact, you and beginning to begin,
    having previously only thought of being.   140

II

You could still become. Consider: from the time that you were born,
    you spent your life preparing to read this book.
(Existentialist laughter is allowed at this point.)
    But admit it: you tried to read philosophy,
that now-desperation of semantics and copulative verbs;   145
    then history, the documentation of forgetfulness
endless with war, and politicians grovelling overseas.
    Drama even, though most of life is farce,
and psychology, 'till you started believing advertisements.
    (Science only suggested you travel faster,   150
at the expense of trees and animals you'd only seen in books.)
    But you knew what mattered and wanted to feel you felt,
and so came to me, prepared to pay for the elegant
    consultancy of a good Australian poet.

III

Were you to open either hand to me, I could take 155
    the lines from your palm, place them on
this map, and show you where you've been in Australia.
    Some tracks will be more deeply etched than others;
we both know why. But it's natural at that age to think
    that better best and beautiful are always 160
on the other side of a city, interstate or overseas.
    Local confidence is what you need.
So don't stand lanceolate and lovelorn, uncertain, confused
    and edge-on to a sun of possible life.
Remove these opercula yourself, and watch: 165
    your season will emerge and stamens-up to flower,
happiness will face you as freedom the released prisoner,
    and possibility will infloresce in everything.

IV

Every problem is a sales opportunity.
    (Here I hope to sell you to yourself.) 170
You've come this far and with your life, so you've written quota;
    the rest of life is bonus, cashable now.
Use the money to travel, young, while you've something to see.
    Play a musical instrument, read classics,
work hard at what you love, and when in doubt, love; 175
    honour commitment, as I and it honour you.
For this advice I expect nothing, but receive everything,
    (how else should I value your approbation?)
They say, wrongly, that writing is the lonely occupation,
    yet I hear your friends clamouring outside, 180
demanding their share in this, the life we want to live.
    Convinced? I am. Shall we sign here? (My pen).

V

For the final stanza, you determine form and detail.
    Decide how much more needs to be said,
and to whom. Edit out the adjectives,   185
    cut in half, wait three days, then post.
If reading aloud and to an audience, prepare.
    Some will tell you that anything easily under-
stood cannot have significance. Ignore them.
    I say watch the barman near the door;   190
if he stops cleaning the glass, leaving cloth and hand inside,
    if neither he nor anyone else is moving,
then you are finally with yourself and all your subject.
    This respect, which cannot be bought, makes
friends of colleagues and acquaintances, and satisfaction.   195
    Treasure this. What else need I say?

The Relevance of Everything

Let me summarise the argument so far: an Australian
    is anyone with a line of me in memory.
Memory is the joy of having experienced what's left of anything,
    or despair of ever being able to stop its destruction.   200
Imagination is a thinking dream thought awake,
    itself deliberate desire to pursue, or allow,
happiness or unhappiness. Therefore you should either
    be more happy, or less happy, than you could ever have imagined.
If more, correct me, but it's a sadder happiness, isn't it?   205
    The sort that envelops the man recalling his outlived
son and daughter, both old and successful in their terms and times.
    If less, again correct me, but it's a happier sadness,
isn't it?   That radiates from the face of a woman who finds,
    unposted, a letter from her long-dead mother,   210
the communication reading her as much as she reads it:
    '... I am what you make of me, and yourself.'

Salute

While I have this breath, your eyes and a glass of wine
    I'll propose these toasts to my Australian readers:
'More final drinks than John Norton' ("never again ...   215
    today"); 'more farewells than Nellie Melba'
("be I ever so humble"); 'more retirements than Henry Parkes'
    ("marbled, high and on a pedestal"),
and hope to enjoy the numberless and obviously to be
    continued adieus, godspeeds, goodbyes and goodnights   220
that serve such good excuse for food and wine, the only
    things of significance overlooked
in this unusual and rewarding alphabet.
    I depend on you for cheddar from King Island,
olives from Griffith and red wine from the Coonawarra   225
    because I best give joy to those of you
who, recognising something of yourselves in every-
    thing I write that is in any way
immortal, want to pay me, and before I die.
    Your poet, Timoshenko Aslanides, thought   230
of you, many even before you were born and,
    except for the bureaucrats and academics
who waste so much imagination trying to come
    between us, wholeheartedly approved!

Notes

Advertisement

The palindromic Greek epigraph to this poem is translated at line 43. The first, second and fifth 'letters' of the 'riddle answer' to this poem (my surname) are from the following 'surrealist alphabet', as remembered by my father-in-law, Ron Stewart (*b*. 1920):

> A for horses (hay for horses), B for mutton (beef or mutton), C for highlanders (Seaforth Highlanders), D for ential (deferential), E for Adam (Eve or Adam), F for vessence (effervesence), G for police (chief of police), H for respect (age for respect), I for Novello (Ivor Novello [1893–1951], popular composer), J for oranges (Jaffa oranges), K for Francis (Kay Francis, actress), L for leather (hell for leather), M for sis (emphasis), N for a dig (*infra dig* abbreviation of *infra dignitatem*, L. beneath dignity), O for the garden wall (over the garden wall), P for a penny (pee for a penny), Q for a song (cue for a song), R for mo (half a moment), S for you (as for you), T for two (tea for two), U for films (*Universum Film Aktiengesellschaft*, German film company), V for France (*Vive la France!*), W for a bob (double you for a bob — one shilling, or twelve pence, predecimal Australian currency), X for breakfast (eggs for breakfast), Y for God's sake? (why, for God's sake?) Z for breezes (zephyr breezes).

22 Wilhelm Brahe was attached to the Burke and Wills expedition, for which see the note to line 7 of 'Imagination', below.

32 *Cooper's Creek,* strictly, Cooper Creek, is a river which flows from south-west Queensland through to the north-east of South Australia. A section of Cooper's Creek, from its source down to its junction with the Thompson River, is also the Barcoo River.

34 The Diamantina River in western Queensland was named after Diamantina Roma, Greek wife of Sir George Ferguson Bowen [1821–1899], the first Governor of Queensland and, later, a Governor of Victoria. He wrote three books, all about Greece, including *A handbook for travellers in Greece* (1854).

Barcoo Rot

According to Sidney J. Baker in *The Australian language,* Barcoo Rot was originally 'a sickness characterized by vomiting after food was taken especially suffered by shearers because of heat, sweating and prolonged bending ...'. The term has been more generally used since about 1870, though, as a synonym for scurvy and Judith Wright told

me that she remembers it as referring primarily to the occurrence of
pustules on the backs of the hands.

6 The springtime it brings on a lot more than the shearing, from the
title and first line of the folk song

> *Oh the springtime it brings on the shearing,*
> *And then you will see them in droves,*
> *To the west country stations all steering,*
> *A-seeking a job off the coves.*

24 Samuel Marsden [1765–1838] was a clergyman. As a farmer, he
was praised by Governor Philip King as 'the best practical farmer
in the colony'. In his capacity of Magistrate, he was generally
known and hated as 'The flogging parson'.

25 and *26* Sir Alfred Stephen [1802–94] and Sir Redmond Barry
[1813–1880] were judges.

26 Mary Ann Brownlow [*c.* 1830–1855] was hanged by Sir Alfred
Stephen for killing her husband. The case aroused a lot of bitterness at the time, not least because men convicted of killing their
wives often had their death sentences commuted.

43–44 The *Georgina, Diamantina, Thompson* and the *Cooper* are
rivers in south-west Queensland.

45 Oodnadatta is in South Australia, 1100 km north-west of Adelaide.

Confidence

5–6 Andrew Murray ('Boy') Charlton, one of our most renowned
swimmers, was born in Sydney in 1907. He subsequently turned
to farming, taking up a grazing lease near Goulburn in NSW. He
died in 1975.

29 Robert 'Long Bob' Spears, cyclist, was born in Dubbo, NSW in
1893 and died, in the Paris he had long loved, in 1950.

Death

33 Hotel Kurrajong, Ben Chifley (Prime Minister 1945–1949), lived
in this centrally-located hotel near the old Parliament House, both
while Prime Minister and later as Leader of the Opposition (his
wife Elizabeth refused to live in Canberra, preferring to stay in
Bathurst).

It seems that he lived on the ground floor, in Room A1. This large bedsitting room with two double-hung windows adjoined the dining room on the south side of the semicircular driveway that swept up to the main entrance. Behind a door on the north wall and in a small niche was an ensuite facility consisting of a handbasin in the centre, and on the left, a toilet and right, a shower.

41 Jubilee Ball, This celebrated the 20th Australian Parliament and 50 years of federation. It was preceded by a State Banquet which Ben Chifley attended and addressed.

76–78 I don't fear death ... it's the form death takes I'm afraid of is a quotation from Ovid:

> nec letum timeo, genus est miserabile leti
> (*Tristia*, I, ii, 51)

101 Another Woman, Phyllis Donnelly, secretary to Ben Chifley was also his lover.

Ethics

28 John Batman [1801–39], pastoralist, sailed from Launceston in Tasmania on 11 May, 1835, to explore the land around Port Phillip. 'This will be the place for the future village', he wrote on June 8 after sailing up what is now the Yarra River. He had previously explored and, as he noted in his journal on June 6, 'purchased', some nearby land:

> *I purchased two large blocks or tracts of land, about 600,000 acres, more or less, and, in consideration there for, I gave them blankets, knives, looking-glasses, tomahawks, beads, scissors, flour &c., and I also further agreed to pay them a tribute or rent yearly. The parchment or deed was signed this afternoon by the eight chiefs, each of them, at the same time, handing me a portion of the soil: thus giving me full possession of the tracts of land I had purchased.*

Fire

3–4 Charles Conder [1868–1909] and Frederick McCubbin [1855–1917] were artists of the 'Heidelberg School' of Australian painting. Conder left Australia aged 21 to go home (to London) in 1890; he subsequently went to Paris, where he enjoyed his part in the *belle époque* and where W.B. Yeats wrote 'after our own verse, after the faint mixed tints of Conder, what more is possible?'

10 Eucalyptus leucoxylon is also known as the South Australian Blue Gum.

11 Salvation Jane, *Echium plantagineum*, also known outside South Australia as Patterson's Curse, is an introduced weed.

13 The Mt Lofty Ranges are in South Australia, where they run some 300 km north-south, 23 km east of Adelaide.

Happiness

17 Lawrence Hargrave [1850–1915] was arguably the most imaginative 19th century aviation pioneer in the world, with interests in, among other things, inventing, exploring, history and marine archaeology.

18 James Swain was a neighbour to Lawrence Hargrave.

19 anchoring rope to a beach, the monument on Bald Hill in Stanwell Park and that famous photograph by Charles Baylis (staged after the event beneath palm trees near Hargrave's house at 'Hillcrest') long gave me and, I expect, many others, the false impression that Hargrave's 'flight' on 12 November 1894 occurred above Bald Hill, or nearby. In fact, it took place on Stanwell Park beach where good winds, the absence of trees and the ready availability of sand for purposes of temporary ballast, were ideal.

Imagination

2 William Bligh [1754–1817] was Governor of New South Wales 1806–1809, which includes a period from 26 January, 1808 when he was held under arrest by Major George Johnston of the NSW Corps.

7 Robert O'Hara Burke [1821–1861] and William John Wills [1834–1861] were leaders of an expedition which intended to cross the continent of Australia from south to north and back again and to explore the interior.

8 Dame Nellie Melba [1861–1931] was the professional name of Helen Porter Mitchell, coloratura soprano.

38 The Perturbator, John Macarthur [1767–1834], soldier and pastoralist, was also known as the 'Botany Bay Perturbator': he apparently once boasted of having had a part in the removal from office of every Governor from Hunter to Macquarie.

Jenny

4 Mt Toolbrunup and the Stirling Range are in Western Australia.

Kenosis

In this poem I have tried to reconcile the Platonic idea of the wish to have children as a disguised desire for immortality, with a recent conception of kenosis interpreted from the Bible (Philippians 2:6, 7) that Jesus Christ was prepared to give up 'the insignia and prerogatives of deity' (which must include immortality) in order to share the experience of being man. A parallel to this is a preparedness to give up the poet's proverbial immortality in order to share, with most other Australian men, the joy of being a father.

Letter (an appeal)

This poem is an imitation of 'An Appeal', by Czeslaw Milosz. See *Czeslaw Milosz: the collected poems 1937–1987*, Ecco Press, New York 1988.

51 used to ripen over our heads like fruit, adapted from 'Noon', by Gabriele D'Annunzio, in *Halcyon*, translated by J.G. Nichols, Carcanet, Manchester 1988, p 84:

> *Summer is ripening / over my head like a fruit / promised to me ...*

Nouns and colonial verbs

5 the George's River takes part of its rise in the hills above Campbelltown near Sydney, flows past Cabramatta and empties into Botany Bay.

9–22 John Macarthur [1766–1834] and his wife Elizabeth [1767–1850] lived at Elizabeth Farm, then a property of up to 850 acres. The house, at 70 Alice Street Parramatta on approximately one acre, is administered by the Historic Houses Trust of New South Wales. Fine merino sheep were initially kept at Elizabeth Farm; other sheep producing coarser wools were also kept at a property on 'The Cowpastures', near the modern Camden. John Macarthur was away from the colony on two occasions: first for three and a half years (November 1801 to June 1805); the second for eight and a half years (March 1809 to September 1817).

23 *Shear, and with the classer*, according to M.H. Ellis, George Dowling was 'the only man in the Colony skilled in wool-sorting'.

33 A *rouseabout* is a general hand in a shearing shed.

34 John Robert ('Jackie') Howe [1861–1920] was a shearer, athlete, hotel proprietor and farmer. His record of shearing 321 sheep (eight- and nine-month-old lambs) with blades in 7hrs 40mins on Monday 10 October 1892 on 'Alice Downs' near Blackall in Queensland still stands.

35 *eponymously clad in himself*: at Jackie Howe's request, his wife Victoria made him a special shearing shirt of flannel material, buttoned on the throat, and sleeveless; this 'singlet' style shirt subsequently became known as a 'Jackie Howe'.

37 a *hogget* is a lamb ten months or more old; a *dag* is a sheep carrying dried dung in its wool; a *snagger*, a sheep with tangled and dirty wool.

39 The *catching pen* holds the sheep ready for the shearer.

40 The *table* is where the fleeces are examined by the wool classer; *locks* are waste pieces (which may also be good quality wool).

41 *shoulder-carried*, sheep to be shorn were at that time carried legsforward and by the shoulder from the catching pen, not dragged backwards as is the current practice.

Other

6 Daniel Henry Deniehy [1828–65], his mention as 'brilliant Dan Deniehy' in a poem by Henry Lawson was subsequently used by Cyril Pearl as the title of a biography of this lawyer and journalist.

Quadrilles

A quadrille is a square dance. The music is usually divided into five sections and is often based on popular tunes, or airs from opera. After establishing its popularity at the court of Napoleon I, the quadrille became popular in England after 1815 and, later, at fashionable dances in Australian colonial society. My quadrilles, also in five sections, were written around Reichenberg's *Australian quadrilles*, probably the first music written and published in Australia; they were advertised in the *Sydney Gazette* of Thursday, 28 April 1825:

> Mr. Reichenberg, Music Master, of the 40th Regiment, respectfully informs the Ladies and Gentlemen of the Colony, that he has composed a first set of Quadrilles for Australia, with proper figures adapted to it, for the Pianoforte, Flute or Violin; as also, for a full Band. The same may be had in manuscript, from Mr. Reichenberg, at the Military Barracks; or at Mr. Campbell's, No. 93 George Street, by giving one Day's Notice. Price 6s.

1 — 'The Collingwood Tote'

1 John Wren ('sports promoter and financier') was born in Collingwood, Melbourne in 1871. His famous 'Collingwood Shilling Tote' first opened for business in rented premises in 136 Johnston Street in 1893. The Tote Room was located at the rear of an operational Tea Shop. Including commission earned from tobacconists, barber shops and other 'agencies' around Melbourne, Wren reputedly netted in excess of twenty thousand pounds per year. Although the tote's oper-ation was described by the Melbourne *Argus* of 29 October 1898 as 'done fairly and above board', John Wren was still described by the magazine *Lone Hand* (May, 1907) as 'that pestilent citizen' and by NSW Premier Jack Lang as a 'champion wire-puller'. John Wren died in Melbourne in 1953.

2 — 'The flying pieman'

1 William King ('professional pedestrian' and 'Ladies' walking flying pieman') was born in London in 1807 and died in Liverpool, Sydney in 1873. His walking feats were numerous and sometimes bizarre as the *Heads of the people* reported on 7 August, 1847:

> He walked .... from the Obelisk in Macquarie Place, Sydney, to the sixteen mile stone at Parramatta and back again, in six hours. He beat the coach from Windsor to Sydney, arriving seven minutes before it. He walked from Sydney to Parramatta and back, twice a day, for six consecutive days. He undertook, on one occasion, to carry a dog weighing upwards of seventy [pounds] from Campbelltown to Sydney, between the hours of half-past twelve at night and twenty minutes to nine the next morning; which he accomplished twenty minutes within the given time.

3 — 'The Speaker's Mace'

In the early hours of Friday, 9 October 1891, the Speaker's Mace was stolen from Parliament House, Melbourne. Rumoured to be on exhibition to clients of a brothel said to have operated in Boccaccio House, in Lonsdale Street, the mace was reportedly used in 'low travesties of parliamentary procedure'. It was never recovered.

Tradition

2 Toby Tosspot, or Sir Edmund Barton [1849–1920], was Australia's first prime minister (1901–3). His nickname apparently resulted from his drinking habits.

3–4 the teacher who tipped-off / that train, Thomas Curnow, released from detention in Mrs Jones' *Glenrowan Inn* (scene of Ned Kelly's last stand) was the schoolmaster who stopped the police train from Melbourne, probably saving it from derailment.

8 Charles Sturt [1795–1869] was an explorer.

9 Burke and Wills, see note to line 7 of 'Imagination', above.

Vegemite

Vegemite is a trade mark of Kraft Foods Limited.

Women

1 Caroline Chisholm [1808–1877] was universally known as 'The Immigrants' Friend'.

21 Dr John Dunmore Lang [1799–1878] was a clergyman and politician.

31 Solomon and Levy, or Benjamin and Moses, In its early days, Goulburn, Australia's oldest inland city, was also known as 'little Jerusalem', such was the number of Jewish settlers, and as late as 1871 the *Sydney Morning Herald* could still observe that 'the ten tribes have not been lost, only mislaid into Goulburn.'

32–33 Mary Ann Brownlow, see note to line *26* of 'Barcoo Rot', above.

33–34 the love that knows of nothing left to love is from stanza 7 of 'On the Paroo', by Henry Kendall [1839–1882].

54 Dame Judith Anderson, [1898–1992] was an actress.

58 Marie Beuzeville Byles [1900–1979] author, bushwalker, mountain climber and one of our original conservationists, was the first woman solicitor to be admitted to the bar in NSW.

X-Roads

35 Woden days, the Woden Valley is south of Canberra City in the Australian Capital Territory, so these are any days in that valley (and not just 'Wednesdays'). Woden is sometimes also referred to as the old English 'God of the weather'.

57–58 the child is truly father to the man, adapted from poem I of 'Poems referring to the period of childhood', by William Wordsworth:

> *The Child is father to the Man*
> *And I could wish my days to be*
> *Bound each to each by natural piety.*

Yass

3 Cooma Cottage (now a National Trust property open to the public) was built *c.* 1835 and sold to the explorer Hamilton Hume [1797–1873] in 1839.

5 William Hovel [1786–1875] accompanied Hamilton Hume on the 1824 expedition to Port Phillip (which they were subsequently to confuse with Westernport).

Zeitgeist

ille ego qui fuerim, 'that you might know who I was', the opening words of Ovid's autobiographical poem, *Tristia,* IV, x.

'My life so far'

2–3 The poet Christopher John Brennan [1870–1932] lived in Crown Street in the final years of his life.

5 Akubra is claimed to be a Pitjantjatjarra Aboriginal word for 'headcovering'. The Akubra Hat Company, based in Kempsey, NSW, since 1972, began as a modest fur-cutting business with Benjamin

Dunkerley in Tasmania in about 1872. In 1911, the company was incorporated as Dunkerley Hat Mills, moving to Waterloo, Sydney, in 1919 to facilitate the expansion needed to cope with the demand for its hats. These are mostly made from the downy underfur of rabbits. A small proportion of production is given over to hats made from beaver skins, which the company believes make the finest hats; these, and hats made from a mixture of furs such as hare, muskrat, rabbit and beaver, are usually produced for the American market.

11 John Thomas ('Jack') Lang [1876–1975], politician and Premier of New South Wales 1925–27 was expelled from the Labor Party in March, 1943.

12 Arthur Streeton [1867–1943] was a founder-member of the 'Heidelberg School' of Australian painting.

13 John Shaw Neilson [1872–1942] was a poet.

43 Many ... are the mothers of lyric poets, adapted from Antipater (*Palatine Anthology*, 7.18.6):

$$πολλαὶ μητέρες ὑμνοπόλων$$

(Many are the mothers of lyric poets)

69 And holding the attention of all, and some quite in spite of themselves, a paraphrase of Ovid's

> non opus est magnis placido lectore poetis:
> quamlibet invitum difficilemque tenent.
>
> (Great poets don't require an indulgent reader:
> they hold the attention of the unwilling,
> and those difficult to please.)
>
> <div align="right">(<i>ex Ponto</i>, III, iv, 9–10)</div>

72 PMG, Postmaster-General's Department, now Australia Post.

81 'UNEMPLOYED at last!', the opening words of the novel 'Such is life' by 'Tom Collins', pen name of Joseph Furphy.

90 Gibraltar Rocks is a formation in the Tidbinbilla Nature Reserve south of Canberra in the Australian Capital Territory. See my *Guide to Canberra and the Australian Capital Territory*.

94–95 Hickory Wattle, Broad-leaved Peppermint, Silver Banksia, Apple Box and *Dogwood* are the common names for *Acacia falciformis, Eucalyptus dives, Banksia marginata, Eucalyptus bridgesiana* and *Cassinia aculeata,* respectively.

'Salute'

215 John Norton [1862–1916] was a journalist, politician and newspaper proprietor.

216 Nellie Melba, see note at *8* to 'Imagination'.

217 Henry Parkes [1815–1896] was a politician, freetrader, federationist and premier of New South Wales on numerous occasions.

Bibliography

The following books were important for the writing of this one.

Aristotle, *Ethics*, translated by J.A.K. Thompson, Penguin 1974.
Timoshenko Aslanides and Jenny Stewart, *Canberra and the Australian Capital Territory*, Kangaroo Press: Sydney, 1988.
Timoshenko Aslanides and Jenny Stewart, *Goulburn and environs: a comprehensive guide*, The Olive Press: Canberra, 1983.
Australians: a historical biography, Fairfax, Syme and Weldon Associates: Sydney, 1988.
James Volant Baker, *The sacred river: Coleridge's theory of the imagination*, Louisiana State University Press, 1957.
Sidney J. Baker, *The Australian language*, Sun Books: Melbourne, 1976.
John Batman, *The settlement of John Batman in Port Phillip: from his own journal*, Quest T. Publishing: Upper Ferntree Gully 1985 (facsimile reprint of the W.H. Williams edition, Melbourne, 1856).
R.H. Blyth, (ed. and trans.), *Edo satirical verse anthologies*, The Hokuseido Press: Tokyo, 1977.
————, Haiku, in four volumes, Hokuseido Press: Tokyo, 1952.
Giovanni Boccaccio, 'In praise of poetry', from *Boccaccio on Poetry*, trans. C.G. Osgood, Princeton University Press, 1930.
C.M. Bowra, *Pindar*, Oxford University Press, 1964.
R.L. Brett, *Fancy and imagination*, Methuen: London, 1969.
James Broadbent and Joy Hughes, *Elizabeth Farm, Parramatta: a history and a guide*, Historic Houses Trust of New South Wales: Sydney, 1984.
Elizabeth Barrett Browning, 'Aurora Leigh', in *The Norton anthology of literature by women*, W.W. Norton: New York, 1985.
R.W.B. Burton, *Pindar's Pythian odes: essays in interpretation*, Oxford University Press: Oxford, 1962.
D.S. Carne-Ross, *Pindar*, Yale University Press: New Haven, Connecticut, 1985.
Humphrey Carpenter, *Jesus*, 'Past Masters' Series, Oxford University Press: Oxford, 1980.
M. Tullius Cicero, 'Pro Archia': the speech on behalf of Archias the poet, in *Cicero: the speeches*, ed. and trans. N.H. Watts, Loeb Classical Library, William Heinemann: London, 1955.
————, *De finibus bonorum et malorum*, ed. and trans. H. Rackham, Loeb Classical Library, William Heinemann: London, 1951.
Samuel Taylor Coleridge, *Biographia literaria, or biographical sketches of my literary life and opinions*, J.M. Dent and Sons: London, 1956.
Tom Collins, *Such is life*, Angus & Robertson: Sydney, 1980.
Peter Collins and David Blair, *Australian English: the language of a new society*, University of Queensland Press: St Lucia, 1989.
Roger Covell, *Australia's music: themes of a new society*, Sun Books: Melbourne, 1967.

L.F. Crisp, *Ben Chifley*, Angus & Robertson: Sydney, 1977.
David Diringer, *Writing*, Thames and Hudson: London, 1962.
Keith Dunstan, *Wowsers*, Cassell: Melbourne, 1968.
Irwin Edman (ed.) *The works of Plato* (the Jowett translation), Random House: New York, 1956.
Thomas Stearns Eliot, 'Tradition and the individual talent', in *The Oxford Anthology of English Literature*, Vol II, Oxford University Press: Oxford, 1973.
M.S. Ellis, *John Macarthur*, Angus & Robertson: Sydney, 1978.
Janet Fairweather, 'Ovid's autobiographical poem *Tristia* 4.10', in *Classical Quarterly*, 37 (i), 181–196.
John H. Finley, jr., *Pindar and Aeschylus*, Harvard University Press: Cambridge, Massachusetts, 1955.
Ross Fitzgerald and Mark Hearn, *Bligh, Macarthur and the rum rebellion*, Kangaroo Pres: Sydney, 1988.
L.F. Fitzhardinge, (ed.) *Sydney's first four years*, Library of Australian History: Sydney, 1979.
Eduard Fraenkel, *Horace*, Oxford University Press: 1957.
Herman Fraenkel, *Ovid: a poet between two worlds*, University of California Press: Berkeley, 1956.
Douglas E. Gerber, *Pindar's Olympian ode: a commentary*, University of Toronto Press: Toronto, 1982.
Basil L. Gildersleeve, *Pindar: the Olympian and Pythian odes*, Macmillan: London, 1885.
Ernest Giles, *Australia twice traversed*, Doubleday: Sydney, 1986 (facsimile edition of the 1889 first edition, also published by Doubleday).
B.P. Grenfell and A.S. Hunt (eds) *The Oxyrhynchus Papyri*, Vol XV item 1795, Offices of the Egyptian Exploration Society, London 1922. The *Select Papyri* Vol III, edited and translated by D.L. Page (William Heinemann, London, 1950) contains a more-complete version of the same series of poems (each beginning with a different letter of the Greek alphabet) and presents a more accurate translation of them.
W.J. Harvey and Richard Gravil, *Wordsworth: the prelude — a casebook*, Macmillan: London, 1972.
John O. Hayden, *William Wordsworth, Selected Prose*, Penguin: 1988.
Seamus Heaney, 'Alphabets', in *The haw lantern*, Faber and Faber: London, 1987.
Mary Hoban, *Fifty one pieces of wedding cake: a biography of Caroline Chisholm*, Lowden Publishing: Kilmore, 1973.
Q. Horatius Flaccus, *Satires, epistles and ars poetica*, ed. and trans. H. Rushton Fairclough, Loeb Classical Library, William Heinemann: London, 1978.
Joy N. Hughes (ed.) *The journal and letters of Elizabeth Macarthur*, Historic Houses Trust of New South Wales: Lyndhurst, 1984.
Margaret Kiddle, *Caroline Chisholm*, Melbourne University Press: Melbourne, 1969.

Hazel King, *Elizabeth Macarthur and her world,* Sydney University Press: Sydney, 1980.
Stanley Lombardo and Diane Rayor, (trans) *Callimachus: hymns, epigrams, fragments,* The Johns Hopkins University Press: Baltimore, 1988.
Czeslaw Milosz, *The collected poems 1931–1987,* Ecco Press: New York, 1988.
A.C. Moorehouse, *Writing and the alphabet,* Cobbett Press: London, 1946.
P. Virgilius Maro, *The Eclogues,* ed. and trans. Guy Lee, Penguin: 1984.
———, *The Georgics,* ed. and trans. L. P. Wilkinson, Penguin: 1987.
Eirene Mort, *Eirene Mort's Australian alphabet,* Australian National Gallery: Canberra, 1986.
Barry R. Muir, *Jack Howe: the man and the legend,* B&J Muir: Blackall, 1989.
P. Ovidius Naso, *Tristia* and *ex Ponto,* ed. and trans. Arthur Leslie Wheeler, Loeb Classical Library, William Heinemann: London, 1959.
John Kevin, and Frances Stickney, Newman, *Pindar's art: its traditions and aims,* Weidmann: Münich, 1984.
J.G. Nichols, (trans) *Gabriele d'Annunzio: Halcyon,* Carcanet: Manchester, 1988.
Frank J. Nisetich, *Pindar's victory songs,* Johns Hopkins University Press: Baltimore, 1980.
Gilbert Norwood, *Pindar,* University of California Press: Berkeley, 1956.
Vance Palmer, 'The labour leader: Joseph Benedict Chifley', in *National Portraits,* Melbourne University Press: Melbourne, 1954.
Cyril Pearl, *Wild men of Sydney,* W.H. Allen: London, 1958.
———, *Brilliant Dan Deniehy: a forgotten genius,* Nelson: Melbourne, 1972.
Pindar, *Odes,* ed. and trans. Sir John Sandys, Loeb Classical Library, William Heinemann: London, 1978.
William H. Race, *Pindar,* Twayne Publishers: Boston, 1986.
Reichenberg (Initial not known), the *Australian Quadrilles* (fortépiano version, 1825), in 'Art in Australia', June 1942.
Ernest de Selincourt (ed.) *Wordsworth's Prelude* (1805–6 version), Oxford University Press: 1926.
Ernest de Selincourt and Thomas Hutchinson (eds) *Wordsworth: poetical works,* Oxford University Press: 1967.
Ronald Strahan (ed.) *The Australian Museum complete book of Australian mammals,* Angus & Robertson: Sydney, 1983.
W. Hudson Swan and Olaf Ruhen, *Lawrence Hargrave: aviation pioneer, inventor and explorer,* University of Queensland Press: St Lucia, 1988.
Charles Sturt, *Two expeditions into the interior of southern Australia, during the years 1828, 1829, 1830 and 1831,* Public Library of South Australia: Adelaide, 1963 (facsimile reprint of 1833 edition).
Ruth Teale (ed.) *Colonial Eve: sources on women in Australia,* Oxford University Press: Oxford, 1978.

Catherine Miles Wallace, *The design of biographia literaria*, George Allen & Unwin: London, 1983.
William Walsh, *The use of imagination*, Chatto and Windus: London, 1964.
Robert Wells, (trans) *Theocritus: the idylls*, Carcanet: Manchester, 1988.
Walt Whitman, *Selections from leaves of grass,* edited and with an introduction by Walter Lowenfels, Avenel Books: New York, 1961.
Stephan Williams, *The flying pieman*, Popinjay Publications: Woden ACT, 1986.
David C. Young, *Three odes of Pindar*, E.J. Brill: Leiden, Netherlands, 1968.

¶